'We found class to be fun, fast and invaluable for our pup, Roxy. All her behaviours were explained so no matter what she did, we were never embarrassed. During training we gained insight into dog psychology and how to turn situations around.'

— James and Jessica

'Norman did not sleep at all if he was not in our bed! But at training we learned about pack structure, patience and consistency. Even though the first night was "hell", all was great after that! Without the puppy training advice we would have given up.'

— Mary

'Our outgoing pup Ridley loved to wee in the house and we wanted to learn the best way to teach him. We set rules at home and within three days he was going to the toilet outside.'

— Arthur

'We have learnt how to teach Kuri to *sit, drop* and *come*, as well as understanding what he is thinking. When we first brought him home he was scared of everything, but at puppy training we were shown how to adapt him to new noises.'

— Leigh and Tonya

'We had a great time at puppy training with our Roxie. Pack structure was an important lesson and we learned how to be pack leaders. We were also taught how to identify naughty or dominant behaviour and how to control it.'

— Robert and Allison

HAPPY PUPPY

By Louise Laurens

M

MELBOURNE BOOKS

Published by Melbourne Books
Level 9, 100 Collins Street,
Melbourne, VIC 3000
Australia

www.melbournebooks.com.au
info@melbournebooks.com.au

Author: Louise Laurens
Title: Happy puppy : a training manual for
puppy parents
ISBN: 9781877096662 (pbk.)

A catalogue record for this
book is available from the
National Library of Australia

NATIONAL
LIBRARY
OF AUSTRALIA

Photographs used in the cover, dedication
and pages 132-134 by Tim Bamford of
Portrait House (*www.portraithouse.com.au*)

Illustrations by Bec Wiggins

For my son Parker

Congratulations on your new puppy.
She will bring you many years of
amusement and companionship.
All she will expect in return is a little
effort from you to keep her safe,
healthy and happy.

Your pup's first week at home …

Day 1   The pup is *not* allowed in the house.

Day 2   Okay, the pup *is* allowed in the house, but *only* for tonight so I can get some sleep.

Day 3   The pup is allowed in every night but must stay in the bathroom.

Day 4 (am)   The pup is allowed in every room but must stay off the furniture.

      (pm)   The pup can get on the *old* furniture only.

Day 5   *Fine, I give up.* The pup is allowed on *all* the furniture except the bed.

Day 6   The pup *can* sleep on the bed, but only at the bottom end.

Day 7   *I have lost control!* The pup is sleeping under the covers with me!

Day 8   *Puppy training has to start!*

Does this sound like your puppy?

Dog ownership is an important responsibility, though one that brings with it many lasting rewards. As a professional dog trainer I have had extensive experience in dealing with bad puppy behaviour, and in *Happy Puppy* I hope to impart you that knowledge. With the help of this book, I'm sure you can have lots of problem-free fun with your new friend.

Table of Contents

Foreword

Having a well-trained pup is a bonus for all owners. We encourage new puppy parents to attend puppy training as it lays the foundation for a lifelong relationship.

Through puppy training you will become better educated with pet health issues, such as medicating for worming and when to vaccinate, as well as learning basic first-aid knowledge, which enables you to avoid panic and know what to do if your dog gets a tick or mouths a cane toad.

Puppy training will also help you understand dog pack structure and general dog behaviour, making you confident in handling and restraining your puppy, and in general discipline issues.

A well-behaved pooch creates a calmer home environment: a happy dog equals a happy parent, so everyone wins!

FERNY HILLS VETERINARY SURGERY

About the Author

Before I start let me introduce myself.

My animal career began at the age of twelve when I started five years of volunteering with Horse Riding for the Disabled.

Between thirteen and sixteen years of age, I was a voluntary helper at the Toowoomba & District Society for the Prevention of Cruelty to Animals, undertaking general grooming, cleaning and finding new homes for homeless and abandoned pets. At fifteen, I took on the position of Junior Branch Convenor at the society, and this involved promoting junior membership, preparing a bi-monthly newsletter, public relations (visiting local schools and clubs), and organising fundraisers (dog-a-thons, pet shows, dog washes, and flea and tick festivals).

In year ten I was placed at the RSPCA, Fairfield Branch, in Brisbane for school work experience. During my time there, I assisted the education officer in preparing for and attending school visits, as well as working with abandoned and rescued animals.

Following this, I began working voluntarily on weekends and school holidays at various veterinary practices in Toowoomba, gaining experience as a veterinary nurse. In 1993, after graduating from high school, I began veterinary nursing studies whilst working in a Toowoomba veterinary practice. During my second year of studies I moved to Brisbane, where I worked in various veterinary practices.

I became a Certified Veterinary Nurse in 1995, gained further experience by working as a locum throughout Brisbane and surrounding areas, and spoke at veterinary nursing workshops.

The following year I was employed by Ferny Hills Veterinary Surgery as senior veterinary nurse, where I was nominated for the 1997 Excellence in Nursing Practice Award. While there, I enhanced my veterinary nursing knowledge, became the nurse manager, and stayed working at this practice until 2004.

In April 1996, I completed Craig A. Murray's Dog Trainer Course and became Chief Dog Trainer for Craig in Brisbane, running courses at Mitchelton, The Gap and Albany Creek. Further to this, in October 1996, I completed Craig A. Murray's Puppy Trainer Course and began training puppies all over Brisbane.

In 1998, I qualified as an Enrolled Veterinary Nurse, and followed this by completing my Advanced Veterinary Nursing Certificate in 1999. I completed the Hill's Pet Nutrition–Nutritional Adviser Program in 1998, and refreshed this knowledge in 2000. In early 2004 I received my accreditation in Veterinary Nursing, followed by my Diploma later that year.

In 2005, I volunteered my time to train pups in Queensland for Assistance Dogs Australia.

Louise Laurens
Chief Dog Trainer,
Paws x 4 Dog Training
www.pawsx4.com

Bella was my youngest Rottweiler at the time of printing this book and proved to be my most challenging so far! She has included a few tips for your pup throughout this book.

SECTION ONE:

UNDERSTANDING YOUR DOG

Before we begin talking about training, let me give you a quick overview of dog behaviour, development, pack structure, and relationship to humans.

Dogs and Humans

How are dogs and humans different? Here are some quick (physiological) facts:

- A dog's sense of hearing is four times more acute than that of a human's.

- Dogs eat based on texture, smell, *then* taste.

- Dogs have only 1706 tastebuds on their tongues, compared to the human tongue, which only has 9000.

- Dogs have about seven square metres of nasal membrane, while humans only have about six.

- Dogs have 220 million scent receptors in their noses, while humans only have five million.

Touch is one of the most responsive senses in a dog, making it the most valuable reward a dog can receive from her owner. Dogs have special sensory hairs called 'vibrissae', which are found above the eyes, below the jaw and on the muzzle, that allow them to sense air flow and current, and to determine the shape and texture of objects.

In addition, dogs need a wide field of vision to locate prey. Angle of vision varies greatly from breed to breed. To get this in perspective, consider the following:

- a person may have a field of vision up to 100 degrees
- a pug may have a field of vision up to 200 degrees
- a greyhound may have a field of vision up to 270 degrees

Dogs also see laterally better than they see straight ahead — so they often have trouble finding something that is right under their noses.

Puppy-hood

Puppy-hood, I feel, is the most important time for any dog. The first sixteen weeks of age lay the foundations for life. Puppy-hood is the time when experiences are new and exert a maximal and long-lasting effect on your dog's future personality and temperament. As a puppy parent, you will have to learn what your puppy is thinking to be successful in training. How you raise your puppy will give you an indication of how your puppy thinks and why she behaves as she does — both as a puppy and in later years.

It is important to understand your puppy's breed: each breed has its own level of stamina, sensory perception, size, agility, looks and emotions. We can read most dogs by their body language — ears, tail, head, body posture, facial expression, eyes, etc. However, these can change with different breeds.

When choosing a puppy there are a lot of factors to consider. These include:

- yard size
- the size of the dog
- the amount of time you can spend

with the dog

- the amount of exercise you are willing to do
- how long each day you want to groom your dog
- what training is required for her breed
- whether you have children now or are planning a family in the future
- what you want to achieve with this dog.

Selecting a dog based on your emotions at the time can often end up a sad story. Owning a dog is for life, so carefully choosing a breed that suits your lifestyle makes a big difference. If you are planning a surprise gift for someone you care about, you should also consider the questions above, as this person may have to live with this partner for over ten years.

It is also during puppy-hood that I recommend you introduce your pup to as many different environments and situations as possible — whether it be the train, bus stop, park bench, rubbish bin, post box, phone box, the beach, shops, going out at night and getting used to shadows, drinking out of taps, or making fun of the rain. It is very important that every experience is a very positive one. Never force your pup onto an object; let her take her time to approach it. If your pup is frightened, don't pick her up or talk to her. This will only encourage her to act frightened in the future. Try to ignore your pup until she starts to explore the new situation. Be patient; this may take a few minutes, but it will teach your pup to be confident rather than fearful. And while it is normal for your pup to be cautious of new things, she should not panic.

A well-socialised dog is happier, confident and healthier. Because she has been familiarised with a variety of environments, stress does not become a major part of her life.

Play

Play is very important as it allows a young pup to practise important life skills without adult consequences, and provides both physical and mental exercise. It stimulates communal behaviour, promotes coordination, teaches action patterns and problem solving, and stimulates inventiveness. Play also builds strong bonds of friendship and trust between you and your pup, making her happier, more sociable, less aggressive and far easier to train.

Play affects and moulds adult social behaviour. It sets the tone for future dominance relationships within the pack, and the enforcement of desirable behaviour sets lifelong standards. Desirable forms of play include running, jumping, hiding, dodging, weaving and wrestling — these may get a little rough, but try to keep them under control. On the other hand, wild and uncontrolled play often leads to undesirable behaviour in adult dogs. Undesirable play takes the following forms: constant mouthing, biting, chewing and nipping.

Eye Contact

Dogs use eye contact to assess each other's temperament and motivation before actual physical contact. A higher-ranking dog makes eye contact sooner and holds it longer. In contrast, a lesser-ranking dog is slower to meet the other's gaze and looks away more readily, avoiding direct eye contact. When neither dog looks away and the body language becomes more confronting, it is possible for dog fights to occur.

As I will discuss in the 'Look' chapter in the next section, the look command is a great training tool. You can use it to get your dog to concentrate on you instead of what is going on around her. It is also a tool that you can use when your dog is stressed — get her to look at you, and if you are calm, you can help lower her stress levels.

Pack Structure

Over the past 12,000 years we have transformed the wild wolf into the myriad of domestic dogs we have today. Nevertheless, dogs, just like their wolf ancestors, live in packs. Each pack needs a leader and a pack order — and the leader needs to be strong, dependable, consistent, respected and in control at all times.

Does your pup seem pushy, destructive, and possessive of food or toys? Does she seem to be running wild — growling at you, jumping on you or your visitors, or rolling onto her back for tummy pats instead of doing what you have asked her to do? Are you tired of your new pup chewing shoes or furniture, barking throughout the night, or going to the toilet indoors? Are you the pack leader in your pack?

Puppies can manipulate us to get what they want. And if your pup is not given proper guidance early on she may try to become the 'pack leader'. You have to improve how your dog views the social hierarchy in your pack, and to do this you need to be more determined, more stubborn than your dog, patient, consistent and fair.

CONSISTENCY + PATIENCE = RESPECT

Being the leader means *you* do everything first and put *yourself* first. This means that you eat first, then feed your dog. You go through doors first and don't allow your dog to barge ahead. If your dog is lying down in the hallway and you need to go through, move her — do *not* go around. Likewise, your puppy should have her own bed and should not share yours. This may seem cute at first; but this puts you on equal footing in dog terms, potentially causing confrontations to do with dominance, and possessiveness over the bed. When, as the owner, you demonstrate leadership by varying daily interactions with your dog, she is more apt to respect your wishes. Simply by changing your household routine — eating first, going through doorways first, having separate sleeping arrangements — you will see a change in your dog.

Spending time with your dog is always fun, but remember to do it on *your* terms. When playing games, you decide when to play and for how long. Similarly, when you give a command, give it *once* and make sure you are able to enforce that command. Never give a command you cannot enforce — there is no need to beg or scream at your dog.

Always be the pack leader and you will be rewarded with a happy dog that will be a delightful companion for many years.

CASE STUDY

'Sally'
Eight-month-old desexed female labrador-cross
Problem: Naughty

Sally was re-homed at eight months of age to a family of six. Although she is by nature sweet, her previous owners did not have much time for her and did not attempt any training. As a result, she has a tendency to be very naughty. This did not work for Sally's new family — they always had lots of visitors and needed a well-behaved dog that could adapt to change at a fast pace. So, Sally's owners attended training to learn how to train their new best friend.

The first step was to meet Sally and identify her personality. There is no single way to train a dog, and all techniques must suit the individual dog and owners. I visited with the whole family present — Mum, Dad, Grandma and the three children (aged 8, 11 and 16) — and watched them interact with their new family member. I immediately felt that Sally had landed with a great family whose members all had lots of time for her.

Pack structure was put into place — everyone ate first and went through doorways first. They learnt to be consistent with training techniques and we designed a training plan that we put up on the wall so everyone could do the same training. As training is a joint effort, each family member needed to chip in and reinforce what Sally had learnt to correct her bad behaviours. Each day we set a new target — although everyone was very busy, we made training fit in with each family member's everyday routine. Everyone worked on Sally a little differently, but the commands they used were all the same (e.g. *drop* was 'down', and *give* was 'drop the ball'). Soon, Sally learned to walk calmly on the lead, sit, and drop on command.

The youngest of the family was the easiest target for her — Sally would steal his socks every morning and jump up at him when he was outside. To Sally, stealing the socks was a game as she was chased. So the family's first target became the socks. Everyone was to ignore the stealing and we would introduce a 'station' (which is a safe place, like a large mat or your dog's crate, where she could lie calmly) for her. She was to get attention for good behaviours only.

Once this was achieved, the family began dealing with the second target: the jumping up. The children were taught to freeze if she jumped up and not to scream or encourage her. Mum and Dad would be on hand over the next stage to enforce good behaviour.

The next stage involved teaching Sally to *stay* and *come*, as well getting her to deal with being by herself. So the family had to teach her to play with toys — she was given a 'kong' with peanut butter inside, and she learned to roll and chase it to get to the peanut butter. They also kicked a ball around the yard and Sally was encouraged to chase and start playing with it. This was especially important for Sally, as she'd never had toys — if a toy is placed in the backyard, she may have just ignored it as she has never had one before.

Over the last four weeks the family had achieved all their targets and Sally was responding to everyone.

The final stage involved signing Sally on to attend a dog training course, which ran for six weeks. Each week Mum and another family member would have a go at working with Sally. Over the six weeks, Sally's family learnt how to enforce the commands *heel, sit, stand, drop, stay* and *come*. They were also taught how to work around distractions.

Sally and her new family graduated with flying paws.

Puppies and Children

Pups provide unconditional love and companionship to their family's children. They don't judge or criticise, and are always there to give affection. But although puppies love their family members, they sometimes do not respect them. And it is children who are often the first to be 'bullied' by a new pup. This is because they react the loudest, play all the pup's games, and are inconsistent. In addition to this, children are usually similar in size and height to your dog.

Children spend a lot of time in the dog's environment (such as the backyard) and don't always know how to react around the dog. Did you know that over half of dog bites occur in the home or garden? To prevent this from happening, it is important to teach children how to approach and behave around dogs, and to involve them in the training. It is also important to teach the dogs from the first day how to act around people of all ages.

As the leader of your pack you have to teach children how to stand tall and be bigger and braver than your new pup. Show them how to stand still and not react at all when the pup tries to 'bully' them. If the behaviour continues, you can 'sin bin' your puppy (refer to the Punishment section for more details). By the same token, remember to praise your pup when she plays calmly with the children.

As I said before: your pup needs to understand from day one that she is at the bottom of the pack, which includes the children.

SECTION TWO:

TRAINING YOUR PUP

With the recent increase of dog behaviour problems and attacks, I feel it is important for people to learn how to train and understand their best friend. For instance, it is because of behaviour problems (which include barking, digging, jumping, destructiveness and biting) that around 80 percent of dogs under eighteen months of age are re-homed or surrendered. These problems, however, can easily be avoided if proper puppy training is carried out.

In the following section, I will offer you guidance on how you can train your pet. If, however, you choose to seek out professional training, see Section Five: Professional Training.

Rewards

Dogs sometimes learn things we didn't intend on teaching. For example, if your dog barks when she sees food and you give her food, she will learn to bark when she wants food. She may then learn to bark in a variety of situations, many of them inappropriate, for a reward. This goes to show how important and powerful rewards are in training. Rewards can take many forms — whether as food, praise or patting — but generally a reward must be immediate, consistent and desirable. To some dogs, even negative attention (like punishment) is still attention and therefore a reward.

Expect your dog to regularly test you as her pack leader to ensure you are capable and consistent. But as with all training, you must be **kind, fair and consistent. It takes time and patience to correct problems, and shaping behaviour takes lots of small steps.** Most importantly, reward your dog when it is doing well. For instance, if your dog is sitting quietly, praise her — if she gets no attention from the family, the good behaviour will not be reinforced.

When you start to teach your pup something new, reward with food every time until the pup has the hang of the task. After a couple of weeks, start to vary the reward — don't give food reward every third time as the pup will pick up the pattern. Random reinforcement is one of the best methods of training. Being by changing the food reward with a big praise, and give food every once in a while. The pup will then try every time in the hope of getting food or the Kong or a praise. Remember: random reinforcement is just like you playing the pokies — food treats should not become habitual.

As I said in an earlier chapter, touch is the most important sense in a dog. Dogs that are deprived of touch often grow up to become fearful and withdrawn. In light of this, touch is the most valuable reward a dog can receive. Use it like food: easy tasks get a little pat, harder tasks may get a hug.

Punishment

If you need to punish your pup, you must make sure that it is **immediate, appropriate and consistent**. Owners tend to be better at punishment than rewards and forget to be calm and positive. However, it is important that you have real expectations — especially as puppies can have tantrums, often called 'protesting'.

One form of punishment is 'sin bin'. This is where the pup has time away from the family and its toys and bed area for a short period of time (about five minutes). If you choose to use this type of punishment, do not use their den — the den is meant to be a safe and comfortable place for your dog, and one that she may sleep in. Thus, it should *remain* a safe place and not a place associated with negativity. Use a toilet or the laundry — somewhere small — and make sure there is nothing she can destroy (e.g. remove the toilet roll)!

Ignoring bad behaviour is another form of punishment. This works well if the bad behaviour is gaining a lot of attention Imagine this scenario: your pup likes to steal objects. All the family members get involved in chasing her until she gets caught, at which time she gets a smack. To the pup this is a game — one where a lot of attention is directed towards her. So in effect, the 'reward' of the chasey game could override the smack. In contrast, if this behaviour was ignored, the pup would find it boring and would stop.

CASE STUDY

'Belle'
Eight-week-old female beagle
Problem: Out of control

Eight-week-old Belle was welcomed by her new family: a couple and their five-year-old son. After five days in the house, however, Belle had left Mum in tears. I received a distressed phone call from Mum, who said she'd had enough and that she was ready to give Belle back to the breeder. It turned out little Belle was very demanding and liked to run amok. She did not go outside, was toileting everywhere, was stealing anything she could get her paws on, will only eat if handfed, and cried when people were in the shower or toilet. The family members continually got into arguments, no-one could sleep, and this new pup was destroying the house!

Belle was booked into puppy training starting the next day. The training session ran over a four-week period and involved the whole family.

My first goal was to get the family to appreciate and have fun with Belle. So we looked at all the positives — what can she do well? They all agreed that Belle loved to sit and shake for food.

During the first class we discussed pack structure, crate training and having fun, and on the next day we focused on leisure activities they could do with Belle. The family played, then Belle had time in her crate, and this was followed by more play then rest time. Belle was to sleep in the crate every night. The family started introducing changes to enforce their position as pack leaders.

Week Two at puppy training saw a huge change: the family were enjoying their new member, and Bella seemed to be learning — she could now *sit*, *drop* and *shake*. The family members were eating first, going through doors first, and having family time both with and without Belle. This little pup had learnt the rules of the house.

By the end of training, Belle was no longer out of control. She was walking on a lead, was playing well with other pups, could *roll over* and *come* in addition to *sit*, *drop* and *shake*, was going to the toilet outside, and had stopped stealing and mouthing. Belle had even attended 'show and tell' at the family's five-year-old son's school.

Tricks

Tricks are a delightful way to exercise, train and play with your dog, while also having a real and important role in her life. They can be used to reduce stress and build confidence, especially if your dog is shy. They can also be used as a valuable tool in behaviour modification programs by providing a fun and positive alternative to nuisance behaviours. And most importantly, tricks are a fun way to communicate and play with your new best friend.

BELLA'S TIP:

Let your owner teach you a brand-new trick. Learn it perfectly. Then, when your owner tries to show off, stare back at them and pretend you don't know that trick.

Set yourself up for success by choosing a trick that you think would appeal to you and your pooch. When training, please keep in mind a few important points:

- Keep sessions short, about one to two

minutes.

- Don't get angry or frustrated — try to have fun.

- Timing is critical — reward within one second; reward small steps toward your final goal; and reward with treats and both physical and verbal praise.

- Keep your dog motivated — take breaks after small breakthroughs.

- Only give one command at a time.

Look

Encourage eye contact on command. Move your hand
to your eyes to encourage your pup to look at you.
Say 'look', followed by praise when she looks at your
face. Slowly increase the amount of time your dog
has to hold eye contact with you (e.g. start with one
second, then five seconds, then ten, etc).

Sit

Place a small amount of food in your right hand between your thumb and index finger. Place your hand with the treat directly on her nose and move it towards her tail. Use your left hand to gently guide the hindquarters down — **do not push**. When your dog sits, say your command (e.g. 'sit') and release the food.

Once your dog has mastered this, place the food in your right hand and use your left hand in the same way. When your dog sits, release the food from your right hand.

After your dog has mastered this too, the next step is to say 'sit', and when she sits, release food and give a verbal praise. Gradually decrease the food and increase the verbal praise.

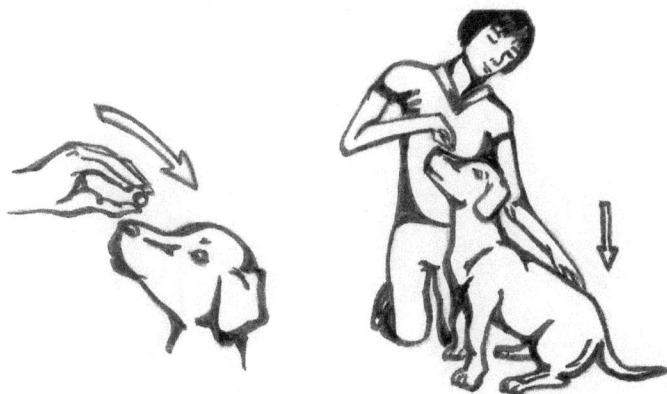

Drop

Place the dog in a *sit* position in front of you. Place your left hand on her collar and the food in your right hand, between your thumb and index finger. With your right hand, swipe out the front legs (from inside to outside), and as your dog lies down release the food and say your command (e.g. 'drop'). Once she has mastered this, the next step is to put her in a *sit* position and simply take the food from her nose to between her front legs and then out in front of her — forming an 'L' shape. Your final step is to ask your dog to drop and praise. Take your time and be patient.

Come

There are four basic rules when teaching the come or recall:

- Have fun.
- Have fun.
- Have fun.
- **Never** punish your dog when you ask her to come to you — no matter what she has just done.

Get down to your dog's eye level, clap your hands and call her name. As she is coming towards you, say your command (e.g. 'come'). Then reward her with food and lots of praise when she arrives.

Remember to keep it fun and avoid making her sit or drop when she comes. Reinforce the training with a little bit of food, lots of praise and cuddles.

If your dog is playing with another dog or something more interesting than you, you have to appear 'more fun'. Try running backwards, using a squeaky toy, or pretending that you are playing a great game by yourself.

BELLA'S TIP:

When your owner calls you to come back in, always take your time. Walk as slowly as possible back to the door.

Shake Hands

Use a piece of food your dog really wants, such as warm roast chicken. Sit her down and kneel in front of her. Hold the food in a closed fist roughly level with her shoulder, and move the hand with the food a little to one side to get her slightly off balance. As she lifts her foot even just a little, use your command (e.g. 'shake') and reward.

Once she has mastered this, use your hand in the exact same way but the treat will be in the other hand. Reward as soon as she shakes. Slowly reduce the treat rewards until you're only rewarding the occasional shake with treats. Make sure you give verbal praise every time.

Roll Over

When your dog lies down, kneel down beside her. Take your treat and place it on her nose, then gently guide it over the shoulder area. Once she is on her back, simply take the treat to the floor. Say your command (e.g. 'over') and reward.

BELLA'S TIP:

When out for a walk, always pick the busiest spot to do a poo.

Take your time. Reward small steps and make sure she is relaxed and having fun. Play around with what seems to work best for your dog.

Walking on the Lead

Teaching your puppy to walk on a lead can be very trying and lots of patience is required.

To begin, attach the lead to your pup and allow her to run around and get used to the weight — ensure that you supervise her so no injury can occur. Try this for five minutes every day for a week.

After the trials, start walking your pup. If she stops, you stop — do not pick her up until she starts walking again. If you recall, owners must be careful to only praise good behaviour, and picking her up when she stops teaches her that she will be carried if she doesn't feel like walking.

Try to avoid patting your pup while she is walking; instead, use lots of verbal praise. Praise her when she is out in front — we are building confidence at this stage. If she starts pulling, simply change direction. Remember to only praise your pup when she is being brave and walking.

BELLA'S TIP:

When out for a walk, choke loudly every time a stranger walks by.

Ignore the scratching at the collar and lead, this is often only protest.

CASE STUDY

Buster
Three-year-old entire (i.e. not desexed) male boxer
Problem: Excessive pulling and aggression on lead

Buster lives with his retired owner, and they spend every day together. They had already attended two previous sessions with other trainers but still were having problems.

I invited Buster and his owner to undertake my training program to help resolve the problem. Buster arrived, alongside his owner, wearing a thick five-centimetre studded leather collar and a 30-centimetre chain lead. After seeing this, I immediately knew what the problem was. Dogs often feel defensive when placed on a short or tight lead, but are relieved when placed on a longer lead and allowed to walk in a relaxed manner.

We began training by taking off the thick collar and short lead and replacing them with a thin correction collar and a six-foot lead. I then worked with Buster on a focus exercise, during which I commanded him to change direction when I did and to then start focusing on what I was doing. Within seven minutes he was working really well. We had five other dogs in this class, but by the end of the class Buster and his owner were walking past the other dogs without pulling.

At this stage, Buster no longer showed any aggression. Later, he also learnt to *heel*, *sit*, *drop*, *stand*, *stay* and *come*, and to work around other dogs and distractions.

Toilet Training

The most successful method to toilet-train your puppy is to den her in a small area — usually a bathroom, laundry or crate (see the next section on 'Crate Training') — so that if accidents do occur, the area is easily cleaned. Make sure you allow your puppy to 'go toilet' after meals, drinking or waking, and always praise toileting in the desired area.

When your puppy is in the den area, you will notice that she will start to indicate when she needs to go to the toilet by becoming agitated, restless or pawing and scratching at the entry/exit ways. Repeat the toilet-training process until you receive the desired effects.

It should only be once your puppy has learned to properly 'go toilet' that she can be exposed to the rest of the house. This ensures there is no chance of making mistakes.

Once your puppy has been allowed into the house, increase the time your puppy can stay in before

BELLA'S TIP:

When you go outside to go pee, sniff around the entire yard as your owner waits. This works well in winter!

putting her back in the den area.

If your pup does 'go toilet' inside the house, just clean up when she is outside. Don't rub her nose in it, and ignore all bad behaviour, as your pup can get mixed signals if she gets attention. This refers back to the 'Rewards' and 'Punishment' chapters (especially the 'stealing the sock' story). If your pup gets a lot of attention when she goes to the toilet inside, she may repeat this behaviour — and both having her nose rubbed in the wee and getting a ten-minute lecture from you counts as attention.

Crate Training

A crate can be used as a den to teach your dog to behave well. This crate must be treated as a special, fun and secure place for your pup, and should never be used for punishment. Associate the crate with positive things — food, toys, blankets, etc. Leave the door open and allow your pup to feel comfortable in the crate. You can throw toys in for her to fetch. Place her dinner inside the crate, and when she is eating, gently close the door. Let your pup out when she is calm and quiet. Gradually extend the crate period.

The crate can be placed anywhere in the house and can be moved.

It is important that she have her own sleeping area or den — it would be ideal to teach your pup or dog to sleep in her den. My dogs sleep all night in their crates, especially as it has been presented to them as a safe, positive place.

Car Sickness

There are many reasons why dogs suffer from motion or car sickness. To address the problem, you must first find out what your dog is thinking when she is in the car. The three most common causes are:

- Stressful experience when a pup
- Negative car experience
- Attention seeking

I will look at each of these a little closer.

By eight weeks of age, a pup will have already been exposed to two possible stressful situations. A pup's first experience in a car is often to the vet's for a vaccination. The second car trip is often when they are split from the litter and suddenly have a new family, home and life — and being split from the litter too early or too late is makes a pup more likely to suffer from motion sickness due to stress. Similar stress issues can also arise if a pup has had incorrect social exposure. If a pup is not correctly socialised into her new environment, that environment will seem very stressful to her. (Refer back to the 'Puppy-hood' chapter for further details.)

A dog may also have a negative experience in

a car that causes subsequent trips to be traumatic. Examples of this are catching a foot or tail in a closing door, or being thrown around in a motor vehicle accident.

Lastly, a dog may get a lot of attention from the family when it is sick in the car. This attention may function as a learning experience for the dog, making her think the family wants her to be sick or that to get extra attention she should 'be' sick.

Retraining your dog is a three-step process that requires lots of time and patience. The first step is to desensitise your dog to a stationary car. This can be done in a number of different ways:

- Play ball in and out of the car.,
- Feed your dog in the car.
- Simply sit in the car with your dog.

As always, ensure that you praise **all** calm or desirable behaviour — even small steps. Repeat this step until your dog is comfortable in the car.

The next step is to start the engine and repeat the first step until your dog is calm (and remember to praise her when she is calm).

The final step is to start moving the car. The first trip may be just down the driveway, after which your dog can be let out. The idea is to slowly increase driving distance. Take your dog to a destination that it perceives is great fun, like the local park or beach. This step may take time — do not push her too far and remember to make it fun and very positive.

One final note. It is a legal requirement in most places to restrain pets when they are in a car or on the back of a ute. This is for safety reasons and will often make your pet feel secure.

Jumping

Jumping is a normal natural behaviour for dogs. However, if she is not taught rules regarding jumping early on, she may think it is okay to jump up on all humans.

When your pup first jumps up, you might think this is cute and pat her on the head or pick her up. Sure, you can take a five kilogram puppy jumping up onto you, but imagine when she grows up and weighs 40 kilos.

Another case is allowing your dog to jump up when you are in your pyjamas, but then getting angry if she jumps up when you are dressed for work. Did you let your dog know when the rules changed?

When your dog jumps up, simply lift one knee and your dog will

jump into your shin; stand still or turn away from her as she jumps. **Do not react or speak to her.** Once she stops jumping up, don't forget to praise her. Also, train your dog to sit or drop when greeting people — a calm dog that is in a *sit* position cannot jump. As always, remember to praise her when she is calm.

Of course, if you want to, you can teach your dog that the command 'up' or 'cuddle' means she can jump up — but keep it on your terms.

CASE STUDY

'Bailey'
Twelve-month-old desexed male Jack Russell-cross
Problem: Jumping

Bailey's owners wanted him to stop jumping. He jumped on the couch, on the family, on visitors, on the car — on everything.

To help solve the problem, the family were shown how to ignore the jumping and reward calm behaviour. In the past, whenever Bailey jumped, the owners yelled at him. As he was getting attention he kept jumping; and the more he jumped, the more attention he got.

Bailey was taught good manners and 'stationing'. For instance, when visitors arrived he was placed on a mat at his station, and it was only when he was calm that he was allowed to come over. At first he had to practise stationing on a lead, but it was not long before he could meet the visitors without his lead. To reinforce the training, the visitors were told to ignore Bailey until he was calm and good.

In addition to this, Bailey was taught how to *sit*, *drop*, *stay* and walk nicely on the lead. This gave the family control and put them on top of the pack structure.

The family now enjoy having friends over, with Bailey enjoying all the positive attention.

Mouthing

In the litter, puppies will 'mouth' each other in a dominance game to see who will give in first. Most puppies continue this game with their new family, as it is their way of sorting out the pack.

Interestingly, puppies do not grow out of mouthing; all you can do to stop a puppy playing this game is to change the rules. Currently your pup begins and ends the mouthing game when he likes. But you should alter the arrangement so that while your pup still begins each mouthing game, it is you who ends them.

When a puppy is mouthing you, simply squeeze the top or the bottom jaw (**not both at the same time**, as grabbing both will cause discomfort and, in some breeds, breathing difficulties) and praise her. Remember: this is still a game. By praising her you are pretending you want to play this game. However, by squeezing

her jaw you're signalling that she is not winning the game, and so she will stop. If your pup comes back harder, you are not playing on her level — you will have to play (squeeze) a little harder.

Don't play tug-of-war games as they can encourage mouthing and aggression. There are plenty of other games you can play, such as Frisbee, chasing and catch.

Digging

Although in most cases owners consider it inappropriate, digging is a normal canine behaviour. In fact, many breeds (e.g. terriers) have been selectively bred for their inclination and ability to dig. The reasons behind this behaviour include:

- hiding bones or toys
- digging bones up
- holes for cooling down or warming up
- digging up prey (e.g. mice) or chasing insects (e.g. crickets)
- to deal with boredom or loneliness
- escaping
- separation anxiety
- lack of physical and/or mental exercise

BELLA'S TIP:

When your owner arrives home, put your ears back and tail between your legs and act as if you have done something really bad. Then, watch as your owner searches both the yard and the house, suspecting that you've caused damage.

To stop your dog's digging, try the following:

- Don't keep garden rules a secret.
- Make sure she has a cool resting place in summer and a warm resting place in winter.
- You may want to provide her a digging pit, and bury toys for her to dig up in this area.
- Look at which parts of the garden your dog has access to when left alone, and fence off 'restricted areas' (e.g.certain flower beds).
- Increase her physical and mental stimulation (e.g. by rotating toys she can play with outside).
- Ignore dug-up holes on your return home — delayed punishment does not work.
- Praise your dog when she is not digging.

Guarding

Guarding, which is where your dog may stand over food, toys, objects, other animals or people, and growl when approached. Guarding may begin as an attention-seeking game. An example of this would be a new puppy stealing objects and running past you attracting your attention. You then chase her and play tug of war until she gives the object back (if at all). It may start with a sock, which may initially seem cute, until her tendency to guard progresses to a bone.

Food aggression is a huge problem, as dogs will guard and defend their bones or other food. Food aggression begins with your dog lifting her lip as she growls at you. This can then escalate to you not being allowed in the backyard at all while she has a bone/

food. A related issue is if children are playing in the backyard and walk past your dog while she is eating — your dog may feel threatened and attack.

Guarding should not be allowed or encouraged. It is vital that you teach your pup from a young age not be aggressive with food. Actively be around her when she is eating her meals and bones, and pat and praise her when she is calm. Every once in a while, take a pig's ear or bone or other treat off her, but remember to give it back and not to tease her with it. Avoid chasing and playing tug of war with your pup when she steals an object or treat and guards it.

If you are having issues with this please seek professional advice as you may be bitten. I would recommend placing your pup on a lead when undertaking this specific training task, so she can not run away with the bone/food. If she runs away, do not chase her — as I said before, she will interpret this as a reward.

BELLA'S TIP:

Wake up 20 minutes before the alarm clock is set to go off and make your owner take you out for your morning pee. As soon as you get back inside, fall asleep. Your owner will find it hard to fall back asleep!

Barking

A dog barking is like a bird singing; it is a completely natural urge and is a form of communication. However, *excessive* barking is a common behaviour problem. To work with this issue it is important to understand why your dog is barking.

Dogs have a number of different barks, each signifying a different reason. Some of these include:

- greeting and communal barks
- boredom
- anxiety (including separation anxiety), fear, stress, feeling threatened
- territorial responses (including disturbances),
- attention seeking (e.g. soliciting play)
- discomfort
- excitement or happiness

Generally, excessive barking indicates that something is wrong with your dog's living situation. And in addition to barking, your dog may also emit whines, whimpers, howls and growls.

There are two steps involved in remedying excessive barking. The first step is to address the underlying issues, and the second is to decrease the frequency of the barking. The aim is to control and modify the dog's barking rather than attempting to get the dog to cease barking completely.

Let's start with the first step. Ensure your dog has plenty of mentally stimulating things to keep her occupied and increase physical activity. Some questions to ask yourself:

- When is your dog barking — which times, days?
- What are you doing when your dog barks?
- What is happening around your neighbourhood?

These questions give you some insight as to the reasons behind your dog's barking. For example, if she barks every morning between 8 and 9 am, it could be because school children walk past at that time. Or if she barks at 11am every day, it could be because your mailman comes at that time.

It might also be a good idea to invest in some toys for your dog, which you can then leave for her to play with when you are out. The toys do not need to be expensive, just fun. You could even make some yourself. A few ideas on what you can do:

- Get an old drink bottle (and don't forget to remove the lid as your dog can choke on it!), cut a few squares on its side and place dry biscuits inside. Your dog will roll the bottle trying to get the biscuits out.

- Buy a giant tug toy and some heavy-duty rope. Attach the rope to a big tree and the toy to the end of the rope. Your dog will love playing with this when you're out.

- You can scatter dry food across the lawn and your dog will spend time finding all the biscuits.

Other tips to help address the *reason* behind your dog's barking:

- Increase physical exercise
- Change your routine
- Take her for a drive when you cannot walk

In the second step, you, the owner, must try to reinforce what you've already taught your dog. People are consistently inconsistent when it comes to barking and often confuse their dog — sometimes the dog is allowed to bark, sometimes it is encouraged to bark, yet other times it is severely punished for barking. Most owners ignore their dogs when they are well-behaved. However, by only paying attention to the dog when she barks, you are actually encouraging the bad behaviour. It's not surprising, then, that many dogs learn that the only way they can get the owner's attention is by barking.

Most people also want their dog to bark when a stranger comes to the front door. This means that barking is okay until the dog is instructed to stop. An example of how you can teach this to your dog is to allow her to bark three times then give a command (e.g. 'leave it') and a sit or drop command followed by praise. A controlled sit or drop can be a very powerful training tool.

If your dog continues to bark, don't shout at her — two wrongs don't make a right. Instead, try and find out the reason behind your dog's barking. For a short-term solution, try using a water spray bottle or a short glass of water in the face (but be wary as this, again, can be seen as reinforcement). Or, break your dog's attention by running around the backyard with a squeaky toy and then rewarding calm playful behaviour.

There is no easy answer with barking as there are so many different reasons and solutions. If the barking persists, the issue might be of the sort that requires you to seek professional advice from a trainer.

CASE STUDY

'Georgia'
Seven-year-old desexed female border collie
Problem: Barking

For seven years Georgia had lived on a sheep property as a working dog, but one day she suffered a bad fall which left her with a damaged leg. At this point, her working life had come to an end.

Georgia was re-homed to a lady who lived in a town block and worked full-time. Her new owner was looking for an adult dog and decided to give Georgia a chance. However, the arrangement left Georgia alone for most of the day, which was a first for her, and even though she had toys she did not know how to play with them — she had only ever played with sheep!

A new environment can cause stress to any pet, with some pets taking up to eight weeks to adjust. In this case, Georgia was suffering stress from facing a new environment and routine, and was bored as she had been used to working. Barking reduces a dog's level of boredom and stress, and it was not long before the neighbour called to let Georgia's owner know that her dog had barked all day.

Georgia's owner decided they should attend training. There, she was told a few changes needed to be put in place to help Georgia adjust. Georgia was to be walked most days of the week with

frequent changes to the route so she could be
exposed to different surroundings. She was to be
taken for drives every night to collect mail, as a drive
gives dogs the same mental stimulation as a walk
and is a nice substitute for times that aren't best
for walking (e.g. when it's raining). Once a week, a
mobile hydrobath person was to come in to break
her day and give her a bath. And most importantly,
she was to be taught by her owner how to play — as
she was food-driven, all her toys had to be based
on food (e.g. the old plastic bottle with holes cut in
it and food placed inside; plastic bottles cut in half
and filled with water; a pig's ear; and ice cubes in a
bucket).

Within fourteen days Georgia was happier and
no longer barked excessively during the day. She still
had a little way to go but was making good progress.

SECTION THREE:

HEALTH CARE

Being a pet parent, you are responsible for your dog's health, so it is important that you are able to perform the following:

- open her mouth and give medications
- clean her ears and eyes
- play with her paws
- clip her nails

As a nurse I used to see lots of dogs just for worming or nail clips. But if you start performing these tasks from your dog's puppy-hood, they will be no big deal when they are required.

Diet

Excellent health begins with good nutrition. And the keys to good nutrition are plenty of fresh water and the correct quantities of a well-balanced diet. For those of you who have forgotten Year Seven science, let me refresh your memory:

- Proteins supply amino acids, the basic building blocks of animal tissue.

- Carbohydrates supply energy.

- Fats provide a concentrated source of energy to meet the increase demands of growth. Fats, along with oils, also promote healthy skin and hair coat.

BELLA'S TIP:

Teach your owners to play fetch. Don't always bring back the stick when playing fetch — make them go and chase it once in a while.

As puppies are still growing, they need to consume more fat, protein and minerals than adult dogs to support the growth of bone, muscle and tissues. These also help to meet their energy needs.

Dried food can be introduced from six weeks of age. I recommend premium dry foods, as they are nutritionally balanced, easily digested and produce less stools.

Raw bones should be introduced at ten to twelve weeks of age, and can be given once or twice a week. **Never** feed your pup cooked bones as they are brittle and can splinter, which could cause choking or serious injury.

Here are some tips:

- Never feed your dog onions, which can cause internal bleeding. Likewise, don't give her chocolate, which can cause heart issues, unless it is specified to be 'dog chocolate'.

- Avoid having your puppy become overweight — a fat youngster may become fat as an adult. Overfeeding your puppy could also lead to diarrhoea, obesity, and a greater risk of bone and joint problems.

- Avoid rich foods and sudden changes in normal diet as this may cause diarrhoea and indigestion.

- Avoid a meat-only diet — meat alone cannot provide all the nutrients your pup needs.

- Avoid giving your pup too much milk or milk products — diarrhoea may develop, and excess calcium can be harmful to her growth

Dental Problems

The most common dental problems dogs experience are dental plaque, tartar, bad breath and gingivitis (or gum inflammation).

Plaque and Tartar

Dogs cannot clean their teeth like we can, and so plaque gradually begins to form on the sides of the teeth. It is a mixture of minerals and salts from the saliva glands, food particles and bacteria. The problem is that once it starts it must be removed as quickly as possible. New plaque builds on old, and soon enough there can be a yellow-grey look and furry feel to the sides of the teeth as tartar builds up.

Bad Breath

Bacteria, the main cause of bad breath, love growing in plaque. And as the tartar pushes back, gum infections set in between the teeth and gums. A friendly lick then becomes no fun at all.

Gingivitis

The reddening, swelling and infection of the gums constitute gingivitis. It is not just the smell that is the problem; the gums retract and cause pain and infection, which will create problems with eating and tooth decay. If things get worse, your dog might even be left with no teeth at all.

What You Can Do

Try to encourage chewing to keep the teeth clean. Strips of raw meat, hard biscuits and raw marrow bones (again: never feed your dog cooked bones!) help keep teeth cleaner.

If you are really keen you might buy your pet their own toothbrush and give the teeth a clean. A wide range of brushes and toothpastes, along with gum sprays, chews, biscuits and toys, are available to aid in the prevention of dental disease.

Bathing

Did you know that the skin and coat of dogs are designed to self-clean? So how often should you bathe your pup? You know she's due for a bath when she starts to get smelly.

Bathing should be a pleasant and fun experience for your pup. Bathing on a cold windy day under the hose, for instance, could lead to your dog hating baths. Take special care to ensure no water go into her ears or eyes.

BELLA'S TIP:

After your owner gives you a bath, *don't let them towel-dry you!* Instead, run to their bed, jump up, and dry yourself off on their sheets!

Avoid over-bathing as it can destroy her skin's natural pH and unbalance its natural oils. Also make sure that you use a shampoo designed for pups instead of human shampoo or laundry detergent as these can further unbalance her skin's pH.

Lastly, when the bath is finished reward your dog with a big towel rub followed by a treat.

Nails

The quick

CUT HERE

Here are some tips on cutting your pup's nails:

- Work under a good light.
- Use clippers that are specifically made for dog nails.
- Avoid cutting into the *quick* (the pink dermis growing at the base of the nail).
- Cut small amounts at a time if you are unsure.
- Make it a fun experience.

If you are unsure about anything, ask your vet, vet nurse or puppy trainer to show you how to do it.

Desexing

What is Desexing?

Desexing is the removal of the reproductive glands to prevent a dog from breeding. In females the ovaries and uterus are removed, while in males only the testicles are removed.

Any dog over the age of six months can be desexed, though six months is the ideal age to do it. Desexing is especially recommended before the female's first heat.

Why Desex Your Pet?

- To help control the dog population and prevent unwanted litters.

- To reduce aggression that results from being on heat, which in turn reduces dog fights.

- To reduce wandering, trouble-making and possible accidents or injuries.

- To reduce prostate problems later on in life in males.

- To stop females coming into heat, eliminating the risk of pyometra (production of pus in the uterus) and reducing the chance of mammary tumours

Myths About Desexing Your Best Friend

Desexed dogs put on weight. Animals only put on weight due to overconsumption of food and insufficient exercise, and this can happen regardless of whether they were desexed or not.

Desexing stops a dog from being a good 'guard dog'. Once a guard dog, always a guard dog — desexed or not. By the same token, some dogs will never be good as watchdogs.

Dogs make better pets if they can have a litter. Dogs have no sense of what might have been — they live day to day, concerned about their daily activities, and they respond in that fashion. Female dogs actually become more aggressive post-puppies, as their protective instincts are aroused, and this arguably makes them *worse* pets for that period of time.

I'd like to make money from having a fertile dog. Breeding dogs is not as simple as having your dog produce a litter. Proper breeding involves selecting a suitable mate, quality food, worming, vaccinations and vet checks, and if you are unprepared you are more than likely to land in debt than make a profit.

Microchipping

Many lost and stolen dogs never find their way home. Imagine coming home from work or from shopping one day, looking in the backyard and finding that your dog is gone. It happens!

Every day, dozens of unidentified dogs are put to sleep in pounds — often while their owners are still frantically searching for them. And a lot of the time, this is due to the dogs not having collars on or losing their tags, which contains their owners' contact information.

Microchipping is the most reliable form of permanent identification. Each microchip has a unique code number that is recorded in a central computer registry. Should your dog get lost and taken to a pound or refuge, their microchip number can be read

BELLA'S TIP:

When your owner arrives home, don't greet them at the door. Instead, hide from them and make them think something terrible has happened to you. Don't reappear until your owner is close to tears.

by a scanner and the owner notified.

Your local veterinary surgery or clinic should have the facility to implant microchips into your dog. Ask their friendly staff for a demonstration of how this procedure works.

Vaccinations

Vaccinations stimulate the immune system (the body's natural line of defence) against disease. They work by training the immune system to recognise and attack the viruses or bacteria contained in the vaccine. Your veterinarian and veterinary nurse will advise you on the best vaccination course for your family pet.

What to Vaccinate Against

- *Distemper* is a viral disease that attacks the respiratory, gastrointestinal and nervous systems. It can cause coughing, conjunctivitis, vomiting, diarrhoea and dehydration. Despite treatment, it can result in death.

- *Parvovirus* is a highly contagious virus that attacks the gastrointestinal tract of dogs. It causes severe vomiting and diarrhoea that both contain blood, which leads to dehydration and can affect the heart muscle. Parvovirus is difficult to treat and is frequently fatal. It can survive in the environment for long periods.

- *Hepatitis* is highly contagious, attacks the liver and is often fatal. It can cause lack of appetite, a very high temperature, pale gums, vomiting, diarrhoea, abdominal pain and general discomfort.

- *Parainfluenza* is a viral disease affecting the respiratory system. It is rarely fatal but can be debilitating. It can cause a persistent infection that can lower the resistance of your dog's immune system. This, in turn, makes her more susceptible to secondary respiratory infections, which can be more serious

- *Bordetella* is a bacterial disease affecting the respiratory system. It is rarely fatal but can debilitate your dog for several weeks. She may develop a hacking cough that often brings up a great deal of phlegm. During this time, she may also be susceptible to secondary disease.

Ear Cleaning

Adhere to the dosing regime recommended by your vet, and follow these steps:

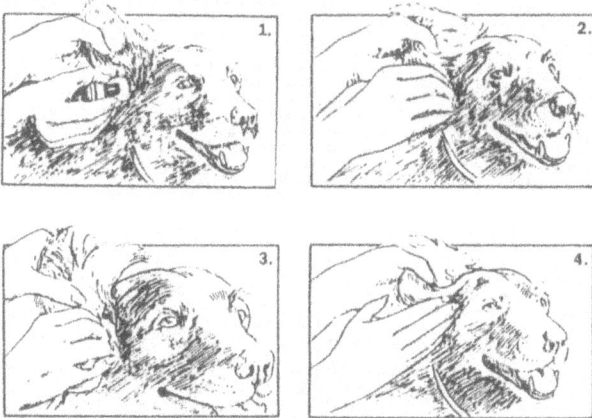

Apply ear cleaner liberally into the ear.

Massage the ear canal by gently massaging the base of the ear.

Place cotton wool over your fingertips and gently wipe the accessible part of the ear clean. Do not use cotton buds to clean inside the ear unless advised by your vet.

Let your dog shake out excess solution and then clean the same portion of the ear again with dry cotton wool. A regular ear-cleaning regime will help prevent infection from recurring.

Giving Tablets

As with ear cleaning, you must follow your vet's dosing instructions. Below are steps on how to pill your dog:

Open your dog's mouth by resting your non-dominant hand's wrist (left for right-handers and vice versa) on her head for leverage, then pressing your thumb and fingers in and upward on the lips behind the large canine teeth on both sides of her mouth. She won't close her mouth because her lips will be between her teeth.

Hold the tablet between your dominant hand's thumb and index finger. Use the other fingers on this hand to pull downward on your dog's lower jaw.

Quickly deposit the tablet on the back of the tongue and then push it as far backward as possible with your index finger.

If you have to dose your dog with more than one pill, an alternative method is to place the pills between your forefinger and middle finger and push them as far down her throat as possible (see inset).

Hold your dog's mouth closed for a few moments so she can swallow the tablet. Don't stroke her throat — this will often dislodge the tablet, with your dog swallowing and then spitting out the tablet. (When I teach owners about this, I normally ask them to imagine swallowing while their throats are being rubbed!) Just close her mouth and wait until she licks her nose.

Intestinal Worms

Dogs can be infected with roundworms, hookworms, whipworms and/or tapeworms, all of which can cause severe damage to the digestive tract. Did you know that around 80 percent of Australia's dogs carry intestinal worms?

Some facts about intestinal worms:

- Hookworms can cause bloody diarrhoea, enteritis, dehydration, anaemia and death.

- Roundworms can cause vomiting, coughing, abdominal pain, colic and stunted growth.

- Whipworms can cause abdominal pain, fever, bloody diarrhoea, anaemia and weight loss.

- Tapeworms develop in fleas and often cause irritation around the anus.

- Hookworm, roundworm and tapeworm larvae can infect children.

- Some worms can produce around 30,000 eggs per day.

- Some eggs can survive up to five years on the ground.

Worming Schedule

How often you need to worm your dog depends on her age:

- *Two to six weeks old*: weekly
- *Six to twelve weeks*: fortnightly
- *Three to six months*: monthly
- *Over six months*: monthly or every three months, but I worm my pets every month as they are around my family.

Your dog should be weighed before every worming, which ensures that the correct dose is given. For example, if your pup is 12 kilograms in weight and the dosage you give her corresponds to the 10 kilogram weight bracket, you have under-dosed and your pup will not be fully covered. As most tablets come in dosages of one tablet per 10 kilograms, it's a good idea to round the dosage up to the nearest half tablet — so in the example of the 12-kilogram dog above, the dosage will be one-and-a-half tablets.

Canine Heartworm

Mosquitos that have bitten dogs infected with heartworm are responsible for spreading the parasite. The disease is found Australia-wide, and because mosquitos are present in most areas, virtually **all** dogs in Australia are at risk of infection.

Adult heartworms cause damage to blood vessels and vital organs. Most owners do not realise their dog has a problem until the disease is well advanced. It is only in later stages, when the disease is difficult to treat, that dogs show the typical signs of advanced heartworm disease: chronic cough, listlessness, fatigue, loss of condition and a distended abdomen caused by the accumulation of fluid.

Heartworm infections can be treated, but therapy is expensive and not always successful. Its effectiveness depends on early detection, prompt treatment and close veterinary supervision. In the final analysis, the best way to control heartworm is by prevention.

Heartworm prevention can start as early as eight weeks of age. **All** dogs over the age of three months should be on daily, monthly or yearly prevention. Heartworm prevention comes in many forms — tablets, chews, top spots or injections.

Before starting on heartworm prevention, dogs over six months of age should have a simple blood test to make sure that they are free of heartworm. Allergic reactions that are occasionally fatal can occur when preventative medication is given to dogs that already have heartworm.

Fleas

Fleas are one of the most common problems encountered by dog owners.

Did you know:

- The fleas you actually see on your pet comprise less than ten percent of the population. The other 90 percent are in the dog's immediate environment.

- Fleas and their eggs can be found anywhere your dog has access to (this may include the backyard, inside, the nature strip, etc.).

- The breeding cycle can be as short as fourteen days.

- Adult female fleas can lay up to 800 eggs.

Flea Control

Fleas can be difficult to control but it can be done. The key to success is aggressive action right from the start. Signs indicating your dog has fleas are skin irritation and frequent itching, caused by the fleas biting and sucking your dog's blood. Hit the flea wherever possible and don't relax just because you haven't seen any for a while. It usually takes one to six months to get a moderate flea infestation under control, and longer if the problem is severe.

Flea control should be combined with environment control. Giving your pet a wash only removes part of the fleas' life cycle: while the adult fleas may have been eradicated, their eggs remain in the environment, allowing them to eventually repopulate. My suggestion is to target all stages of the fleas' life cycle — your vet nurse can advise you on the best product for your particular situation.

Remember to treat every pet in the household all year round. There are several products on the market to treat your pets. There are also sprays and bombs available to treat indoors, garages, kennels and bedding.

Ticks

The paralysis tick can **kill** your dog. This particular species of tick is found wherever there are bandicoots (the tick's main host), and plenty of lush greenery to support both the ticks and the bandicoots. It is particularly prevalent in the warm, wet months but will crop up all year round.

The tick attaches itself to a 'victim' and begins to feed on blood. As it grows and matures it produces a nerve toxin, and by the time it is three days old it will have produced enough to cause clinical signs.

The signs letting you know your dog has been infected by the paralysis tick are:

- Wobbliness in hind legs
- Change in or loss of bark
- Coughing
- Vomiting
- Difficulty breathing

If your pet is showing these signs, she requires **urgent** treatment from your veterinarian.

Ticks are small, difficult to find and hard to remove. The adult paralysis tick is oval in shape, grey in colour and its legs are very close to its snout. You can find the ticks anywhere on your dog's body, but generally they hide inside your dog's mouth and ears, between her toes, and on her face or neck. Because they are so elusive, careful searching is a must.

If you find a tick, do **not** apply kerosene or other irritants to the tick. You can simply pull it off provided you do so quickly. If you are unsure, kill the tick with an insecticide — such as Fido's, Frontline, RID or Aerogard — before attempting to remove it. Do not spray the entire animal; simply apply directly to tick.

As with everything, however, prevention is much better than treatment. There are tablets, collars, top spots, sprays and washes available to protect your pet. Talk to your local vet nurse to find the best product to suit your best friend. That said, when it comes to ticks, no matter what product you choose to use, nothing is 100-percent effective.

Toad Poisoning

Toad poisoning can occur if your dog bites or mouths a cane toad. Cane toads secrete toxic venom through the glands located at the back of their heads. This is then secreted into your dog's mouth and absorbed through her gums and lips. The venom is sticky and white. Most poisonings occur at night or in the early morning, and particularly after rain — but be wary, as it can still occur at any time of the day or night.

Signs and Symptoms:

Signs develop within a few minutes and death can occur within fifteen minutes. Watch out for:

- Profuse salivation
- Vomiting
- Disorientation
- Red mucous membranes (e.g. gums)
- Dilated pupils
- Muscle rigidity or spasms
- Convulsions
- Heart irregularities

First Aid

- Wash your dog's mouth out with cool running water.
- Rub her gums with a washer to remove the sticky toxin.
- Continue washing her mouth for at least ten minutes.
- Contact your vet.

Do not excite or stress your pet while you are giving first-aid treatment, as these can intensify the effect of the toxin throughout the body. Keeping your dog calm will slow down the toxin's effects.

Emergencies: When to Go to the Veterinarian

Any of the following requires urgent veterinary attention:

- Inability to breathe or gasping for breath
- Blue tongue or gums
- Bleeding (from any part of the body) that does not stop
- Vomit, diarrhoea or urine that contains blood
- Inability to urinate or move bowels
- Severe and continuous pain
- Loss of balance or consciousness, coma, convulsions
- Tremors, sudden blindness or unusual withdrawal
- Any penetrating wounds
- Poisoning
- Broken bone/s
- Any injury that has caused lameness
- Heat or chemical burns
- Any signs that you are unsure about but look serious

The following, while still requiring veterinary attention, are not urgent:

- Vomit or diarrhoea that persists
- Sudden lameness with no apparent cause
- Severe itching
- Strange odours from any part of the body
- Excessive urination and/or drinking
- Sudden loss of appetite
- Any injury that you are worried about (e.g. broken nail, cut ear) that doesn't appear serious.

If your dog does suffer an injury, you must make several decisions in a very short period of time. These choices may affect the overall wellbeing of your pet. It is vital that you **remain calm and try not to panic**. Being in pain, your dog may resist any handling and may try to bite you; just be on guard and take precautions to protect yourself.

Do you know what is normal for your pet? What is her normal appearance (e.g. gum colour)? How does she normally behave (e.g. eating and drinking patterns)? Knowing these things will help you determine whether something is wrong with your dog or not.

If you are worried about your pet for whatever reason, never hesitate to call your local vet or vet

nurse and ask for advice.

Shock

If your dog has been involved in an accident or trauma, she can suffer from shock. Signs of shock include:

- Pale-coloured gums
- Shallow breathing
- Cold paws or tail
- Weakness
- Seeming depressed

If you think your dog has undergone shock, try to stay calm, keep her warm, and contact your vet.

Heat Stress

Heat stress is caused by over exposure to heat. Some situations that can cause heat stress:

- Training in the heat without enough breaks
- Excessive exercise during hot weather
- Overexcitement
- Lying in the sun for extended periods during summer
- Being locked in a car

To avoid heat stress, give your dog an ice cube instead of a big bowl of water after a summer walk. Ice cubes can be used as a reward as some dogs love playing with ice. You could even make giant ice cubes: use old drink or milk bottles (and again, remove the lid) cut in half, fill them with water and freeze.

It is also **never** a good idea to leave your dog unattended in a vehicle. Did you know that a dog can die in less than six minutes when locked in a car during a Queensland summer, for example?

If your dog *does* experience heat stress, stay calm, remove her from the heat source, and contact your vet.

Ant Bites

Ant bites usually only cause a local skin irritation. However, as we humans would be aware, they can be quite painful. Signs include:

- Pain
- Itching
- Redness

What can you do to relieve the bite? Apply cold water to the area — for example, if your dog is bitten on the paw, place the paw in a bowl filled with cold water. But if your pet is bitten on the mouth, eye or throat, seek urgent vet attention.

Eye Injuries

Eye injuries are serious and eyesight can be lost within 24 hours of the injury. If you notice your pet has an eye injury, immediately seek vet attention.

Do not:

- Apply cream or ointment
- Remove any foreign body
- Distress the pet
- Leave the injury

SECTION FOUR:

OTHER THINGS

Pet ownership includes a wide range of responsibilities. It is important that as an owner you know your community responsibilities, including understanding the animal local law. Similarly, life can throw both exciting and sad times that affect both you and your pet. A few of these are included in this section to help you understand and prepare, should the need arise.

Expecting a Baby?

This is a very special time in your life, but preparing for this change can be scary. Have you considered that this new bundle of joy could cause distress for the family pet? Try putting yourself in her shoes — she has been around for a while and is used to having the run of the place, when all of a sudden a small person arrives and all the rules change. The pats stopped, the walks stopped, the fun stopped. She is no longer allowed in certain areas of the house, and the small person in question is getting a lot more attention than she is. Other factors also come into play. For instance, the age of your dog can affect her ability to take to a new child:

- Does your dog have arthritis or an old injury?
- Is she losing her hearing or eyesight?
- Can she get out of a crawling baby's way?
- A crawling baby who wants to learn to stand might grab your dog and pull themselves up on her. Will your dog be patient enough not to retaliate from

that?

Changing things gradually will give your dog lots of time to adjust. It is important that you set the structure you want for when your baby comes home. Again, structure is vital in any pack, and your dog must understand that at all times she is below the family — which includes the baby.

Although there is no hard and fast rule about when such training should commence, I believe the sooner you start, the better. It depends a great deal on the individual dog. You can start preparing the minute that you fall pregnant, or you can do it twelve weeks out. Ideally you should have started at least four weeks out.

When the time arrives and your baby is born, bring home a nappy from the hospital for your dog to smell so she can identify with your baby. It is important that you do not leave the nappy on the ground as your dog is likely to eat it — just give her a smell and then you can throw it out.

When bringing your baby home, make the introduction slowly, calmly and safely. Place your dog on a lead and put her into a *sit*, *stay* or *drop-stay* position, then when she is calm and you are ready, show the baby to her. (Refreshing your dog on how to *sit* and *drop-stay* will assist in a calm introduction. If your dog doesn't know how to *sit* and *drop* and *stay*, now is the ideal time to start teaching her.)

There are other simple things you can put in place to limit negative outcomes:

- Place a screen door on the nursery to keep pets out of this room

- Ensure food bowls are behind a baby gate.

- Make sure your dog has a safe place to go when she needs some time alone.

- Worming pets is very important, and as your dog will be around babies, it should be done monthly. Roundworms can cause blindness in children.

- When taking your dog for a walk, hold the lead in your hand. Do not tie the lead to the pram because if your dog runs the other way and the pram flips, the baby could be injured.

We also recommend that any dogs that live with children should go through some sort of training, puppy training and dog training as that can limit future problems.

One last thing. To some dogs, crying is a brand-new noise as they might never have been introduced to a child, so they might not know how to react to it. The baby might have a restless night and this can cause stress for the family pet. Playing a CD* of 'crying baby' sounds will allow your dog to get used to the new noise. As you play this CD, your dog may react to it and start howling. For example, when I was pregnant we played the CD and in the beginning we had three howling Rottweilers. But by the end of a couple of weeks (playing the CD during dinner, while we were watching TV, going in the car and throughout the day), the crying had become an everyday thing to the dogs.

Good luck, and remember:

- Seek professional advice if you have any concerns or issues.
- Praise your dog when she is behaving calmly around the baby.
- NEVER leave any dog unattended with any child or baby

*'Crying baby' CDs are available directly from Paws x 4. To order your copy, please visit www.pawsx4.com.

CASE STUDY

'Honey'
Eighteen-month-old desexed female cattle dog
Problem: Expecting a baby

Honey was the first 'child' of her family, slept on
her parents' bed and ruled the house. But her mum
and dad were expecting their first (human) baby in
six months, which would be a huge change for all
of them. What's worse, they had also just bought a
house and had only lived there for a week. And while
still unpacking, Honey started urinating in the house.

During a conversation with Honey's owners,
they admitted they had not been spending much
time with her. The walks had been cut back due to
the move, and it was obvious Honey was feeling
very left out. I told them that although they needed
to prepare, it was important that Honey didn't feel
isolated from the baby. Instead, they should teach
Honey rules when being around the baby. So we
decided that now would be the best time to change
Honey's routine and prepare for the new arrival.

Honey started crate training inside the house,
and was given an area outside on the patio that
was secure and protected from the weather. We
designated this her 'safe place'.

The next thing was to refresh her training with
sit and *stay*. Honey had attended puppy training but
her owners could not allocate time to attend further
training. Honey picked up *sit* and *stay* really quickly

— being a typical cattle dog, she was very eager to learn and clearly wanted to please her owners, who then rewarded her with positive attention.

A 'crying baby' CD was played at different times of the day to prepare Honey for this new sound. After four days Honey no longer seemed to take much notice. After ten days she did not care at all.

At this point, Mum was up to the seven-month mark in her pregnancy. Honey's crate training was going well, walks had started again and she had adjusted to spending time on the patio by herself. The baby's nursery was almost finished too, and Honey was taught this was a 'no go' zone. Mum and Dad did some work around the house with Honey on lead, including *sit* and *stay* around the doorway of the nursery, and stationed her on a mat in the hallway when they went inside. With consistently enforced rules that didn't leave her out, Honey was back to having fun and enjoying her new home.

Once the baby was born, Dad brought a dirty nappy home for Honey to sniff. This preliminary introduction made the actual introduction go a lot easier — Dad placed Honey on a lead and in a *sit* while Mum held her son in her arms. Honey sniffed his feet, seeming very relaxed, and then went into her crate and watched every movement.

It is sometimes quite hard to keep positive and focused. But most issues are trainable — Honey and her family worked through the issues together and are all really happy it worked out.

Holidays and Your Dog

A lot of work goes into planning your annual holidays, but what about arrangements for your family pet? In theory, leaving her at home and having a neighbour look in and feed sounds ideal. But being home alone for long periods can lead to a change in behaviour patterns, with excessive barking or an escape plan posing potentially big problems.

There are two ways to avoid this: the first is to send your dog to a reputable boarding kennel, and the second is to opt for pet-friendly accommodation.

Boarding Kennels

Kennels, like any other business, are run in different ways, and what appeals to one person may not attract another. Do your research early and find the perfect pet retreat. Things you could do include:

- Look in your local directory for nearby kennels.
- Check with your vet and friends who have dogs.
- Make appointments to visit all the kennels and see what each one has to

offer.

- Ask lots of questions — you can never ask too many. You must feel comfortable with the boarding kennel you decide to leave your dog with.

Most kennels welcome your interest and will be keen to let you see how things are run. They want your business and, most importantly, they want you to return year after year.

Once you have found just what you are looking for, keep the kennel's business card in a safe place. Then, when the time comes around for your next holiday, book in early. Remember: as with your own holiday bookings, the best accommodation is always booked up first.

It's a good idea to book your dog into kennels for an occasional short mid-week or weekend stay. This will not only help her get to know the kennel helpers; it also gets her used to being away from home and knowing that you will be back to collect her soon. (Though this, unfortunately, cannot stop her from missing you terribly.)

Pet-friendly Accommodation

The alternative solution is to take your family dog with you. Pet-friendly accommodation is becoming more and more popular. There are a wide range of holiday rentals available, with some resorts offering garden apartments where your dog is very welcome and high-rise apartments accommodating small breed dogs. If you decide to take this option, you will need to know the phone number of your nearest vet clinic — just in case there is an emergency.

In addition to this, barking and other bad behaviour will not be tolerated within the premises. I would suggest taking a crate with you— crates fold easily, and can be used not just for sleeping but to confine your dog if you have to leave her inside for a short while. Just remember to leave the radio or TV on for company.

As with kennels, do your research early and you will find everything so much easier when holiday time approaches.

One last thing: make sure your local council registration is up to date and, of course, that your best friend is microchipped. Whether at home or on holiday, it's always worthwhile taking precautions in case your pet goes missing.

Council and Your Pet

As a responsible pet owner it is important that you understand your council's local laws and abide by them. Local animal laws are designed to both protect your pet and keep your community safe.

It is important that you ensure your dog does not create a nuisance to the neighbourhood. You can do this by ensuring that:

- You have your dog under control at all times
- You attend training
- You pick up your dog's poo
- Your dog cannot go under, over or though your fence (even just her head)
- Your dog is not barking excessively
- Your dog is registered with your council
- You understand your local laws

Dealing with Pet Loss

The human–dog bond dates back to over 10,000 years ago. Pets share our lives and our affection, but sadly there will come a day when we have to say goodbye. The death of a pet is devastating, and people deal with it in very different ways. Grief is normal, and unfortunately there is never an easy answer.

A pet passing away is especially significant to children. Children often develop strong attachments to dogs, particularly if she was the child's first responsibility. Doing a good job can increase self-esteem, and losing the pet can be a disaster for a child.

The death of a family pet is often a child's first exposure to death and can provide a lifelong imprint. Children grieve differently to adults and understand death differently based on their age. They may be very sad one minute, then playing and happy again ten minutes later. Following a pet's death your child may show other behaviours, including nightmares, aggression, and bedwetting.

It is important that you discuss your pet's death honestly with your child, reassuring him or her that grief is normal and that it is okay to express it.

My son was almost three when we lost one of our dogs unexpectedly, through illness. It was a week before his third birthday. I was not sure how much he understood; however, every night he would ask to go outside and sent a kiss to the stars. On his birthday he said that our dog must not have loved him as she did not say happy birthday before she went to heaven. This made me so sad.

I was advised by the doctor to create a photo magnet of her and placed it on the fridge so he could talk to her. This really helped. We talked about losing pets and what happened to them. A year later he would still come up and ask for a cuddle and would say he was sad. I told him this was normal and that I was sad as well. I believe it is important to encourage children to express their feelings even though sometimes it is very hard for us to listen to them.

Dogs are a huge part of our life and even when we have lost them they are with us every day. We never forget their funny ways, making us smile when things remind us of them.

However, if you are experiencing grief-related issues with your child please seek professional advice. Your local doctor can advise you further.

SECTION FIVE:

PROFESSIONAL TRAINING

There's more than one way to train a dog, and as the owner you have many different options to choose from. One of those is profession dog training. The most common dog problems I see include lack of socialisation, discipline and basic commands (e.g. sit, drop and come), toilet training, mouthing, biting, chewing and destructiveness, but with training you can make owning a dog more enjoyable.

If you decide to enrol your dog into training, don't forget to enjoy the experience. After all, training should be one of the best things you and your dog get to do together.

Choosing Training

As I said earlier, dogs living in a family 'pack' need to respect their pack leader. As a pack leader, your dog will love you, truly respect you and wish to work for you on your terms. If you do not assume the position of pack leader, your dog will be under the impression that you are subordinate to her. Your dog will then believe that she can behave as she pleases. There are many tools at hand for dog owners to gain this respect, and one of these tools is dog training.

Dog training is designed to educate you and your pack about how and why your dog thinks and behaves. The trainer you take on works for you, and it is important that each lesson is designed to cater to your individual needs. Every person and dog is different, and there are many ways to train a dog. If a technique is not working for you, your trainer should offer you other ways or ideas.

Before starting training, some questions you may ask the trainer include:

- where and when they were trained,
- whether they attend any ongoing training,

- what equipment they use and why they use it, and

- whether they have any references.

Unfortunately, there are people who will try to portray themselves as professional dog trainers but skimp on equipment and ongoing training. If they do this to themselves, will they do the same with your dog? I strongly recommend that you check out your local dog trainers, interview them, and if at any time during training you are unsure, ask questions.

Paws x 4

Paws x 4 is Louise Laurens's foray into the world of small business. It started in 1996 and under this banner she educates future dog and puppy trainers by running programs for the public at various venues throughout greater Brisbane. Paws x 4's mission statement is to provide total and ongoing commitment, care and dedication to owners and their well-trained best friends.

Paws x 4's training programs are designed to train *you* to train your dog in a way she will understand. When training dogs we look at the normal behaviour for their breed and identify any problematic behaviours. It is important that owners understand their dog's breed, as different breeds have different stamina, sensory perception, size, agility, looks and emotions. No breed is superior or untrainable

It is important that your trainer finds out about you and your dog. Some questions you may be asked when attending a Paws x 4 training session include:

- How old was your dog when you brought her home?
- Why did you choose this one?

- What do you want to achieve at training?

Questions like these will assist Paws x 4 to work out a plan for you and your pet.

Paws x 4 offers **free** pre-purchase advice and behaviour modification, and conducts lectures, seminars and workshops for owners of both dogs and puppies.

Puppy Training is designed to socialise your puppy and educate you, the parents. Paws x 4 offers a four-week course designed for puppies under 16 weeks of age which covers socialisation, basic commands (*sit*, *drop* and *come*), pet care information and puppy problems such as toilet training, mouthing, biting, chewing, destructiveness and discipline.

The Paws x 4 Dog Training Course runs for six weeks, during which you will learn how to control your pooch with exercises that include the *heel*, *sit*, *sit-stay*, *drop*, *drop-stay*, *stand*, *stand-stay* and *come* commands. You and your pooch will learn how to work around other dogs, people and distractions, as well as having   lots of fun.

How to Photograph a Puppy

1. Unplug camera from charger.
2. Remove charger from puppy.
3. Turn on camera.
4. Mount camera on tripod.
5. Find puppy and take sock from mouth.
6. Place puppy in front of camera.
7. Return to camera.
8. Crawl after puppy on hands and knees.
9. Take camera off tripod.
10. Focus with one hand and fend off puppy with other hand.
11. Remove nose print and slobber from lens.
12. Catch cranky cat and put outside.
13. Bathe the scratch on puppy's nose.
14. Put magazines back on coffee table.
15. Try to get puppy's attention by squeaking toy over head.

16. Replace glasses and check camera for damage.

17. Jump up quickly, grab puppy, and run outside.

18. Call partner to help clean up mess.

19. Go get a drink.

20. Sit back in chair.

21. Book puppy into puppy training tomorrow.

Good luck and remember to have fun!

Louise with an Assistance Pup during a training session.

Top: Bella as a pup (eight weeks old) with her favourite toy.

Bottom: Max and Bella at home, in Burpengary.

Bella, Max and Tess at feed time.

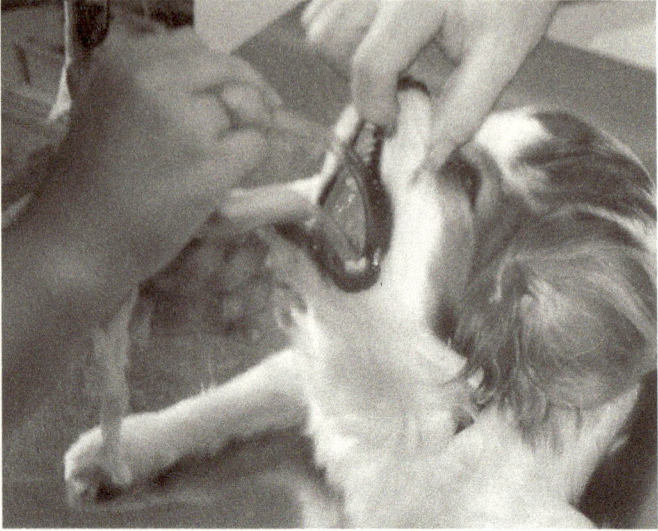

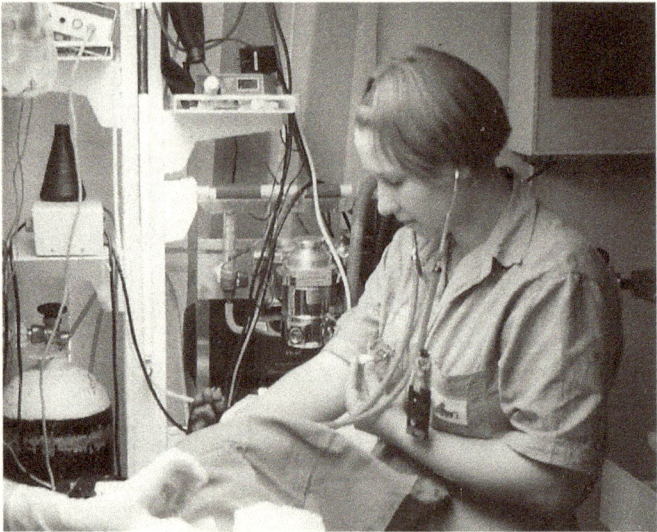

Veterinary Nurse Louise giving medication and in surgery at
Ferny Hills Veterinary Surgery.

Parker as an infant, with Max and Bella. While my dogs are fully trained and well-behaved, they are still kept on a leash with minders (not pictured) watching over when around infants.

Teaching Porsche *drop* and *drop-stay*.

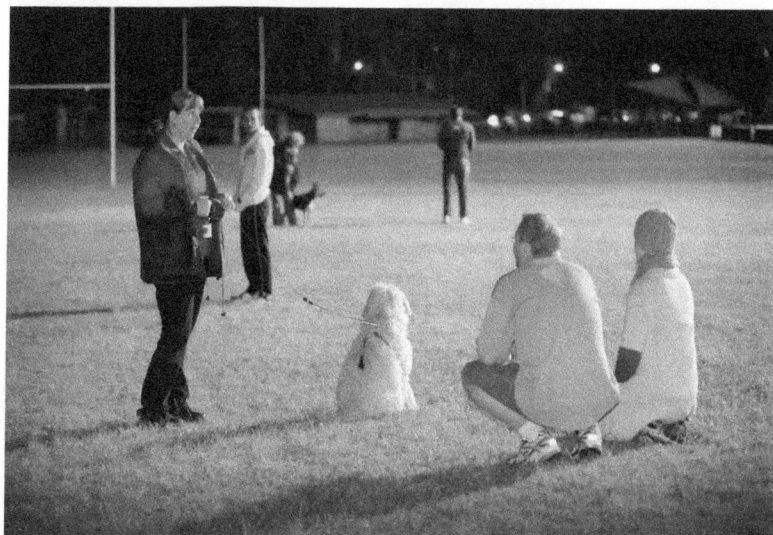

A dog training class at Mitchelton.

Louise's son, Parker, as Junior Pack Leader, learning new puppy tips.

www.ingramcontent.com/pod-product-compliance
Lightning Source LLC
Chambersburg PA
CBHW030942090426
42737CB00007B/502